Satya Mohanty is a poet, playwright, novelist, and writer. A former officer of the Indian Administrative Service, he served as Union Secretary of Education and as Secretary General of the National Human Rights Commission. An Edward S. Mason Fellow at Harvard University and a SPURS Visiting Scholar at the Massachusetts Institute of Technology, he has also taught economics as an adjunct professor at Jamia Millia Islamia and Guru Gobind Singh Indraprastha University, Delhi.

Mohanty has authored a book of essays in Odia, A*aina Michha Kuhena (The Mirror Does Not Lie)*; two earlier collections of poems in English, *Dancing on the Edge* and *Migrants' Chronicle & Pandemic Musings*; a book of plays, *Breathless & Other Plays*; and a work of non-fiction, *Unpolitically Correct: The Politics and Economics of Governance*. A regular columnist on economic and socio-political issues, he is fiercely proud of his role as a public communicator. He lives in Hyderabad.

Harvesting Gods

Poems

Satya Mohanty

SPEAKING
TIGER

SPEAKING TIGER BOOKS
125A, Ground Floor, Shahpur Jat, near Asiad Village,
New Delhi 110049

First published by Speaking Tiger Books 2025

ISBN: 978-93-6336-843-9

10 9 8 7 6 5 4 3 2 1

Typeset in Adobe Garamond Pro by
SŪRYA, New Delhi

For my daughter Sukanya—
Let your words grow
to paint the universe in colour

CONTENTS

Preface

POETRY VERY OFTEN is intertwined with the divine and the sublime. To evoke experience, emotions and insights requires a creative power greater than the ordinary—a palpable grace that enables connection with the unfamiliar, stirs the flow of insights and pierces the heart of the reader like an arrow. Ultimately, poetry should awaken deeper understanding and gently lift the veil on hidden truths. Without these sacred qualities, poems remain verses written on bits and pieces of paper, which fly away.

This book has taken shape out of disquiet and unease, often bordering on restlessness; both my own and the world's. The poems here are born from watching closely, listening carefully, and often, grieving silently. They are my way of grappling with questions that refuse to stay still or disappear.

Harvesting Gods metaphorically symbolizes the gathering and realization of experience, insights, knowledge and wisdom—which gods represent. This harvesting is not done with a scythe, as the image of harvest usually conjures up, but like the gentle picking of grains by birds from the pods. Poems under the sections titled *The Desire, Uncommon Communion, Half Deserted Street & Muttering Retreat* and *Hope Not a Tattered Flag* will broadly fall into this category.

I did not set out to write a book around themes of gods, desire, memory or nature. They arrived unbidden, like unrelenting visitors at my door, asking to be given voice. Over time, I began to see that they were not separate conversations but part of one long dialogue—between the self and the world, the past and the present, the visible and the invisible. The gods I write about are not always celestial beings. They are also our creations, our fears, our justifications. They appear in town squares and parliaments, in temples and streets, wherever power claims the language of divinity. *Harvesting Gods* is a critique of power and authority, where the more powerful always harvest benefits from others. Poems under *Miasma, A Country with a New Name, Climate Poems, Upside Down Poems* explore this dimension of the rubric. Be they gods or an enemy, they are there to harvest and twist narratives to a tale of triumph. We are made to "brew the elixir of the past for concocting the future" in the process.

Desire, too, runs through these pages, not as ornament but as question. Ancient epics taught us that longing is both creative and destructive, and my poems return often to that paradox. Desire is fire, but it is also memory's lingering smoke. It is what pulls us toward another, and also what drives us toward art, toward truth, toward transcendence. Writing about desire, I found myself writing about human fragility and the strange beauty of our cravings.

The poems on nature and climate emerged from a deep unease. I have walked hills that no longer stand whole, seen rivers choking on our waste, watched cities sink under their own ambitions. In these moments, language feels inadequate, yet silence feels complicit. Poetry became a way for me to mourn but also to remind myself—and perhaps you—that the earth is not a possession but a gift, which is alive and wounded and speaking back to us if only we care to listen.

This collection also wrestles with memory—personal and collective. I have seen how histories are rewritten, how myths are polished into weapons, how silence is imposed where voices once thrived. Against that tide, I wanted to record, however humbly, a testimony. Sometimes it comes out as lament, sometimes as resistance, sometimes as nothing more than a stammer. But even stammering is a form of speech, a refusal to vanish.

If these poems sometimes seem weighty or burdensome, I hope they also carry their share of light. For even in the darkest images, I have tried to hold onto hope. But hope here is not about ignoring despair but about surviving it, pushing back against it. Like roots breaking through stone, it insists on life. When darkness blossoms all around, we require our area of dignity and hope. We cannot afford to have a world marked by diminished dignity or loss of hope. Poems under *Hope, Not a Tattered Flag* position us between the starshine and morning—a necessary bridge to look ahead.

I offer this collection not as answers, but as invitations. You may find echoes of your own doubts and longings here, or you may find provocations that unsettle you. Either way, my hope is that these poems will linger, not as finished pronouncements but as burning questions and quivering truths.

Miasma

God

God is a lie
that flowers our fear.

In his name,
the invisible hand
becomes a crushing grip
to smother the "other".

Ayodhya

Now all squares are roundabouts,
all streets dead ends,
every junction is a maze.
History is uncoiling itself
like a slouching beast from stony sleep.

Picture the town in reverse,
domes bulge, spires vanish,
memory dims but pulverization stands out.
The blood-red tide of people
swells like raging sea waves
chanting of conquest,
conflating consecration
with just reparation.

Where is forgiveness then?

Bhoomi Pujan

Search the earth, Ram will spring.
Why Ayodhya, but in any stone or twig.
Why Hindus? In any faith you choose.
You only need devotion
to metamorphose stones.

Devotees make the divine.
Not the manic monsters
or scheming politicians.
Temples can't be built
with royal pride or golden bricks.

You make melodrama your staple diet
but God does not descend with burlesque.
Mime is worse than hollow reverence,
it will only be easy to lose faith
and impossible to acquire it.

False History

You combine the watermark of fables,
potshards of odd findings,
and an arcane dream of a long-lost past.
To stir a translation of a temple,
you took disenchantment for truth.

Temples have been broken down
piece by piece to build a stupa.
Viharas broken to build proud mosques.
But like rain lilies
leaves become tubers, tubers become flowers,
only to vanish with decay.
Demolition is not at heart,
the smudging of identity is.

Desire: A Quintet

Questions: Wrapped in Mystery

"Desire is the essence of life."
– *Mahabharata*, Canto XII

Is desire a pleasure?
A fulfilment like spring harvest,
a part of "becoming"
the sky of compressed blue,
sought for and craved as
the horizon opening its mouth
to savour and satiate?

Does desire etch your destiny?
Like a road with missed bends
and gaping meanderings?
"Will" created in a bush of fire.
"Action" a meaning-packed journey?
Destination as enchanting
as a brief crack of light
between blankets of darkness,
a spirit to break free,
leaving the harbour behind.

Does desire hinge on completion,
full and lasting
as an endless exuberance,
or an anticipation of the good, great and lovely,
of allure and grace
which decants into timelessness?

Or, is it endless pain,
a sure recipe for suffering,
where getting burnt
will not alchemize virtue?

Pandavas desired one woman.
In private, five brothers lusted one,
coiled like a snake
it sprung open
to slither forward
for war, revenge, death and annihilation.

Senses move to imagination.
A ladder to the empty field of sky.
Fantasy, the promise of a blooming garden.
Pleasure comes from flowers playing,
buds bursting open,
to create a deluge of colour and scent,
with memory as green as the stalks.
After they die, what next?
Ashes of boredom,
difficult to salvage from and
impossible to fly in the arc.

A Road to Nowhere

"There is melancholic sadness
at the very heart of Kama."
– *Mahabharat* 1.85: 7–8.

I

Desire, the beginning of torment.
A yearning which the arrow unleashes.
Be it of white or blue lotus,
or of jasmine, ashoka or mango,
only to be marinated in longing,
skewered in lust,
and to be soft-charred in waiting.

What if desire turns into intent?
Never mind determination and action,
but it puts you under the enchantress' thrall.
One tethered to the object,
cravings for the things desired
as disconsolate as unquenched thirst,
once satiated, a new craving starts
slipping forward
from the snakeskin of habit.

Antelopes get lured to their death
by songs.
Moths fall into flames
attracted by their beauty,
fish swallows the hook
being avid of flesh,
desire, a passage to destruction
by desiring to desire.

Manmatha's arrows of flowers
create simmering longing.
Burning lust,
an illusion of what is not,
like the reflection in still water.
A snake, a fowl and a pig
go in circles.
Each biting the tail
of one in front,
heedless of their own.
A go-around in radiant discontent.

What if desire leads to delight,
delight, the fountainhead of discontent
because after fulfillment what remains?
An endless unmutating misery?

With one impaled by desire,
desire of lust and love,
desiring to live forever,
desiring to be reborn to savour all,
where is Nirvana after all?

II

Two lovers swear by each other
of infinite passion and endless love,
the vow they take of an undying union.
After a year of fire and
thirty years of ash,
there are curdled dreams,
the vows are expired cheques
no one bothers to encash.
"Everydayness" ate the promise up.
Who was lying more or
who was lying less?
Where is the truthfulness?

While talking to one,
the man looks desirously at another,
thinks of the third.
Where does his mind dwell?
Now or there or nowhere?
Where is the mindfulness?

Two people break up.
One is making tender speeches,
is he still in love?
Was the girl not in love
or the reverse?
The tiny conspiracy of double-speak,
where lies the real?

The more you feed,
the craving grows like a hippo's,
the bigger it becomes.
The man about town had all the arts.
A clear success in every way.
But his mind moved away
after keeping the trophy in the closet.
Now he lusts for someone else.
What remains of tenderness now?

The princely son of a kingly politician
with swag and all,
he is the moon of someone's eye.
Without him, the other will die.
Now he is desiring another.
To have one more debit card,
for what he has feels like a dime or nickel.
Eros has loosened his limbs
and weakened his mind.
Where has steadfastness gone?

The arrow was tipped with desire
laced with anticipation.
Feathered with longing,
necked with resolve,
it pierced the heart.
But uncertainty remained,
the darkness of the unknown,
what will unfold
what will fade?
Is the roller coaster ride a given
or is it a journey on a potholed road,
where efforts are incommensurate,
with unknown achievements,
a fate of ravishing disappointment.
Where is the certitude then?

They are like wild horses.
The charioteer can't lose control.
To be torn in many directions,
as a surging river
floods the plains of sanity.

Remembrance of Things Past

"Even now,
I remember her eyes,
restlessly closed after love,
her slender body limp
fine clothes and her heavy hair loose –

I shall recall her in my next life
and even at the end of time."
– *Caurapañcāśikā* (*Fantasies of the Love Thief*), Bilhana

I

Desire, is it the mind or body?
It is the body swinging to nature
and mind, the cosmos, conjuring up the past,
long stacked away somewhere.
Sage Vipul controlled Ruchi's senses,
held her back from Indra's lure.
Remorse dogged him, haunted by the intimacy
of hunting psyche,
guilty that his vows were compromised.

"Smara", the name of the god of love,
handsome and bodyless,
stirs desire through memory,
across the simmering remembrance
of things once loved.
Bilhana, facing death,
redeemed his love with memory,
sure that he can recall her image,
beyond death and
at the end of time.

II

Ancients called it "smara",
meaning both memory and love.
Memory becomes an editor,
arrays events, experiences and people.
Events sewn together
but which were not met earlier.
The half-deserted street
becomes chock-a-block,
people all around become a hazy glaze
like the smog-laden sky.
Experience rises from ashes of derangement
to a patterned tapestry, recollection
reshuffles the past by the customised present.

The alchemy of recollection
subdues the chaos,
arranging in pattern
what never happened
or remained half-spoken.
Is it the same person,
remembered with minutiae enhanced
or just the mystery of Eros?

III

They just signed the papers,
inked their separation, walked away
and were glad that it was over.
Falling in love,
going through blissful nearness
was so easy.
But "somewhere" staying in it was difficult,
boring, mundane and insufferable.
It felt like being in fetters.
Gnarled teeth and raised voices
were the torturous diurnal.
Thank God, it ended what had to.

The memory of all the talks
in the days of light,
the long walks without purpose,
tiny reckonings and boundless gestures,
the beauty of togetherness
still surface in flashes
until everything soured.
It is the "maran" both had to go through,
dying of love,
a death that killed the best in them.

Strange Thing About Being a Renunciate

"Men do not praise souls driven by desire,
Yet, in this world, there is no activity which is free from desire."
– *Kamagita*, Book XIV, *Mahabharata*

The renunciate abandoned
life's fun, frolic and pleasures,
decades of enjoyment
he earlier felt would not be enough.
"Vairaga", he thought.
A straight walk into the dreams,
the "moksha", the salvation
of the earthly soul.

He abandoned the Kama tree,
anger and ego, its main trunk,
ignorance at its root,
twigs of anxiety and branches of sorrow,
fear in the buds,
and creepers covered with longing.
He renounced attachments, separated from desire,
practiced austerities,
to distance himself
from the "maya" of desire.

What is the reality then?
Desiring not to desire,
desiring not to be reborn,
are they not desire then?

II

Did he meander into it?
Was it a hasty calling?
Or an anticipation gone sour?
The more he denied desire,
the desire grew,
with remembrances of the past
mixed with new longings.
Will he ever meet his maker?
Where is the deliverance,
when darkness has swallowed his path?

III

From friends, he has moved
to dark echo chambers.
He has forest, rocks and darkness around.
A cold bed and bone-chilling wind.
No consort to warm his bed.
In the bewilderment of love
he has moved to a wasteland,
where the same silence

he meets every day.
Same trudging and difficult climb,
same thirst and hunger,
same body aches and hurting wounds,
but no one is there
to nurse him or care.

IV

His jagged pain,
his tangled roots,
don't take him to God any closer.
A dispensable object
in God's schemes.
God has appeared not even once.
He did not want words, he wanted life,
a life that dances with the day.
When the body becomes ashes,
how can it return?
He longs desperately,
for people to come and friends to join,
consorts to frolic
and the world to know.

From Eros to Agape

"Desire is powerful indeed, it engenders itself."
– *Remembrance of Things Past,* Marcel Proust,
translated by C.K. Scott Moncrieff

I

Bodhisattva felt the suffering
of living creatures around.
Nirvana awaited him
without the pain of rebirth.
A compassionate one wanted to be born
to free all beings alive,
in the escape of birth and death,
the never-ending cycle of *samsara*.
This desire was deep-born
to help and do good to others,
not for his own sake,
but a *philia* where others only matter.

II

Denied desire only grows,
a weed unattended.
The renouncer will be reborn

to fulfil the desires unfulfilled.
How does he conquer desire?
Use desire to conquer desire.
Let Kama be a ritual of which no residue will be left
to torment ever.
Guidance will be to liberation,
a pure moksha.
Strange that salvation comes
through the exuberance of Kama.

III

We search for the sacred,
we yearn for the divine,
we try to do the highest good.
Desire affirming life,
liberation is the human breath,
an extension of nature.

What in the end is beautiful?
Liebstod, the love death,
the sacrifice through love,
transcending all that decays and dies,
escaping being victims of fate,
a triumph over the mundane,
a final proof of freedom,
love fulfilled in death,
a proof of freedom,

a redemption never reckoned.
"Welt Atems Wendhem All."
Salvation reached
with "I" dissolved,
a refusal to renounce
the passion; or futile the world may say.

IV

The gopis desired Krishna,
their path to heaven,
their connection to enlightenment,
there was no *tapas* or meditation,
there was no need for austerities.
It was no longer a fickle attachment,
no revulsion or boredom to ensue,
no cinders and ashes after consummation.
Love and beauty flowed,
it was sacred and cosmic life force
far away from fleeting love.
Krishna cannot be possessed;
Radha suffered the pain
when she tried.
The love envelopes the gopis
in a sphere of protection,
the circle of love of God.
What if one stays in love,

there is no imprisonment here,
love is liberation,
without the malefic "maran".
There is peace, quiescence and dissolution
of the self in immersing in Krishna.
There is no rebirth after this.

V

When desire is a pleasure itself,
when it is sacred and unspoiled
by "dailiness" of relationship,
where it is in the right balance
with *artha, dharma* and *moksha*,
where duty to myself flourishes without hurting others,
where desire embraces the divine,
the barrier between love and spirit crumbles
to make one an erotic–ascetic
without the love of the world being thwarted,
let me seek my desire with the earnestness of bees.
When thirsty, I want water,
not the finest of wine.

Uncommon Communion

Creation

Vowels digging into
thickness of clouds,
deepening and thickening at whim.

Consonants rippled across
and froze into a languor.
They seemed to have gone back
where they all started.

Both consorted at twilight
to quicken me to the verb.
An active verb without longing,
but the mellowed clarities
enveloped me like the
darned plunge line of radiance.

Breathless

Breath, the whisper of the living,
purifying, audacious and elemental,
just decided to descend
from a cube of light to
a space where no lamps are lit.

A lunge for a little bit of sky
while feinting to avoid that catastrophic kiss,
which the air swerved down to the plant.
In a time unrecommended by event,
when the ether is lambent with deadly stillness,
this will end with carrion kisses or carrion farewells.

Otherside

We sailed our ships close to the coast.
Caution saved us from perdition,
the homeless moon shone all through.
The sea roared and raged.

The anchorless pestilence
raved and swerved
coming down to give a fateful kiss.

We managed to swing away,
once rigged for a long journey
in the turbulent sea.

A reprehensively perfect life was not our pole star,
a desire for oblivion guided us
to where we headed on the other side.

Harvesting Gods

What if the crops failed,
jobs dried up as a dying river,
and the economy shrunk like an ageing man,
losing in three dimensions,
God is always there to be harvested.

What if the spin of yarn is a tangled knot,
a great mess-up or a territory lost,
soldiers killed by the incursers,
enemy is omnipresent as God
helping to twist it into a tale of triumph.

What if our present looks violated,
in the crowded halls of arrivals and departures
of social media,
we would finally be brewing the elixir of the past
for concocting the future.

Upside-Down Poems

Dharma Sansad

Sansad was real,
dharma was an alibi.
We moved away carrying hatred home
just like mother cats carry their kittens.

God was killed there
when the speakers with saint-like looks
spewed venom from their ghostlike souls.
Can God reside
where hate reigns?

Those moth-eaten airs
were the rancid breeze
flowing from another world,
hiding today in yesterday.
So that tomorrow can
be buried in today
in the sharp teeth of
unproved belief.

Stammer

The rendezvous my words have
these days
is with the death, dead and dying.
Once they met during
spring, fall, rainbow and sunrise.

Gods have become
the vanishing Saraswati,
lost in the sand of prejudice.
But they don't wait to surface
lest they face pitch darkness of belief.

The gulf between the word and the deeds,
is it a stammer or lameness?
But it has become the lingua franca
of people intoxicated, enticed and enthralled.
They can no longer escape
the sharp tooth of existence.
It is no longer a metaphor.

Witnessing Cataclysm

Images stumble,
smiles limp,
voices are drowned,
light has faded.
We are born unto disgrace.

If you sleep among convicts,
you can't wake among angels.
Chasing your God is fine
until you start chasing out others.
Then edification and death are the same.

Languages of storm don't
make people Jehovah.
Speeches of prophets
don't lead people to redemption.
There could be flowers but no fragrance in the end.

Doubts dubbed as philistines
when unalloyed devotion was being asked for,
but they didn't know others
when they are called the shadowed ones.
As a witness, I am drinking
only poison now.

Unknowing

They descended the hill
like a flock of white sheep.
They didn't look like snow melting
but resolute like the sheepish dogmas
they harboured in confidence.

Did they know themselves?
Did they know what they were up to
while sanctioning food,
lynching men and stopping love from taking root?

Can you know yourself
if you are in thrall of "I"?
How can they know others
when they are called "them"?
Their journey ends at the door of silence,
inside they have no idea.

The World Is Turning Blind

A man died saying
"an eye for an eye
makes the whole world blind."

Can revenge turn the wheels back,
wind down the history
as if all is even?

No way will it be even,
past can't be steamrolled today,
nor can yesterday be hidden in tomorrow.

The stench of the past seduces your nose
with the overpowering taste of having no other.
The brain has become a tongue, flickering and devouring.

People lived and died
by the light of that day
but with the light we received
we have gone blind.

Climate Poems

A Requiem to Hills

Men stomping the holy land,
cars speeding on the outflow of asphalt river,
built with trees cut, hills razed and gorges filled.
Tunnels bored like gouging out innards
while skyscrapers come up like nimbus clouds.

The earth rumbled,
rock plates shifted,
rivers rose in revolt in full spate.

Mother Nature says,
"I am not your keepsake chattel,
not a prize for your good karma
to be used at whim."

Tragedy at Uttarakhand

The sky trembled,
the earth rumbled,
the river was in spate.
Clouds pregnant with peeves finally burst
wiping off all signs
of the living, liveable and lived.

"Thousand dying lives is no curse."
People reasoned
about what nature wrought.
Nature paused and asked:
"Is living many deaths finally a blessing?"

A Map of Wretchedness

We barely knew about perdition.
We had trust in the constant tenancy of man,
the moon with no home was out of the equation,
completely, almost completely.

Highways to nowhere,
fancied in conceit,
look splendid in desolation.
But the earth disembowelled
is a hollow barrenness waiting to explode.

When evening lights no lamps,
we hear a choir of echoes,
the moon goes raving
in a valley empty of life and death
boldly drawing a map of wretchedness.

Joshimath

Katayan king Vasudev of lore
cut the undercover Narsingh's left hand.
The wound spewed milk, not blood
but the icon got a weak southpaw.

When his left hand fell,
the rule of the line ended.
While Joshimath sinks
what will come to an end?

What will Badri do
without the staging post?
Will he be in endless wait for the devout,
now that trails of easy travel vanished?

A hundred and eight gods
robbed a goddess;
Mother Nature, the sustainer.
Freeways, hotels and tunnelling underneath
made the goddess cry in anguish
and she just cursed to sink the town.

Sunrays will fall
on a flattened Joshimath,
land no longer will mean
strips of shadow and light,
but a scar on the earth,
deserted and barren.

Dirge to Nature

Wait a bit, I have not finished yet.
This is something in which merely milking words will not do.
Nor will hunting for metaphors or gathering similes.
Even burnishing with haunting images or lilting pastorals
may not do the job.

We must start with the beginning:
another, or this one or the one we always believed
to unravel what we have seen and heard.
Or what is yet to happen
to herald another kind of knowing;
to know that we are not wholly dead
but usherers of empty life foretold.

The rumbling earth and trembling sky
we mistook them for
rattling of washer-dryer of laundromats
or the plate-glass clatter.
The quotidian markers of our lives.
But nature had become a wound
from which the present world flowed.
Our suffering congealed
where roads widened, bridges were built
but nature, like flowers, wilted.

Was it part of the perfect murder
high on impact, low on trail?
It didn't require anything perfect
except taking away as much as you can.
Silent sobs and muted howling
clobbered under unsubtle perfection.

Development-wallahs thought the door to be a gate.
They danced to the music,
without honouring abundance.
They fast-talked well-being
hiding their sins in cheerful smiles.
We hardly knew that the tune had changed,
driven mad by the splendour of their vision.

Now the truth is upside down.
Memory is a curse
that does not ever stop flowering.
Our punishment is
unuttered but continuous
in the ruins we inflicted.
Hills imagined our sufferance
in the quelled restiveness of night and dark.

In the morning, mourning pours with sun rays.
Birds are fewer and air is lambent ugliness.
Finally, we have maimed our song.

Nature's Lament

Now, I am a forlorn hand-me-down.
It was not meant to be like this.
Taken on loan,
I should have come
with so many add-ons,
improved, enhanced and better.

You will see me
aching and empty of life and death.
No, maybe more of death
even if life still throbs
to tell the story,
the story of happenstance or prodigal mishap.
I come violated, grieving and unrecognizable.

A Country with a New Name

Death of Civility

Streets gurgled into the rooms,
long thought to be omphalos
of being sane and civil.

Not the sharp-nosed men with faces dirty,
bad teeth or quick-shifting eyes,
but mind twisted and thoughts contorted.

Oozing along like
a cracked sewage pipe
and trickling still,
we are caught in the little pond
where dregs have parked,
in water smelly, putrid and deadened,
where lily can never bloom
or no fresh air will waft across.

No Earthly Colour Will Change

(Based on the Hathras incident)

No earthly colour will change.
She is dead, her voice silenced forever.
The grass is limp with damp.
Nothing can hurt her anymore.

No colour changed,
her tongue was slit.
Even the hasty incineration can't hide
the bleeding silence of the time.

No colour changed
when fingers dug into flesh.
She hated her mouth sealed by mouths,
hands pinioned, her body still like carcass.

No colour changed,
when the clear tears hung like melons.
No fantasies but a muffled outcry
of violation fraying her apart.

No earthly colour will change.
They didn't need a hideout, vastness was an ally.
Karma was hidden with countless collaborators.
Justice drowned in traffic; a quicksand of forgetfulness,
it was a past buried in the future.

Our World

It was a long and narrow road.
He didn't walk down
to meet us,
not halfway even.
We had to walk up
but when he wanted to meet.

We knew not
that we have invented our doom,
like scoundrels we clung
to patriotism as our broom.

There is thieving in the alley,
lynching in the valley,
as the rain beats down,
cranes fly away,
as the stars fall down,
sanity cries away.

A wicked world it has become
as Sodom and Gomorrah.
When he walked on the cloud,
our dreams got twisted
with his glib talk
and manipulation of the crowd.

We met Satan as a man of peace.
We thought we saw tenderness in the beast.
Now only crickets talk in rhyme,
in staccato, we are more or less done in.

A Country with a New Name

Weeds of yesteryears
come back as fresh bloom,
we accept a future which is ancient.
In an air
lambent with belief
we allowed them to imagine us.

Hatred is the ambience now,
hatred for others,
hatred for the self,
hate for everything around.
Love has gone on a Sabbath
when bare hands became fists.

Gangsters are in power,
lawbreakers make rules.
Killers are declared martyrs
and sinners become angels.
We find neither night disappearing
nor the dawn nearing.

When we stride as wise men,
we come back as fools.
Astrology trumps economy,
hocus-pocus of stars
surge ahead of truth.

Finally, truth is an unknowable stuff,
what we get
is profoundly impure and too obscure.
Devotion is the code of the road.
Will there ever be a judgement on the predators?

The Oracle

I

With a saint-like face and ghost-like soul,
ghoulish thoughts and macabre turns,
eyes cold like quiet running water.
Underneath, snakes playfully slither.

II

How many myths to be created
to make the humans demons?
How much of history to be defaced
for truth to be suborned?
Lies fly with abandon,
truth comes only limping after,
it was after all cruelly buried under vaporous cant.
While history was forgotten on a whim.
Myths shift from hand to hand,
eye to eye,and they become resplendent as Gods.

III

Stories catapulted into orbit
only go round and round.
The Oracle invents science
when none exists,
spins yarns of tales and narratives.
We quiver on the edge of real answers,
when they regale beyond the closed door of myths.

Generals' Failure

How will you atone
for failures as big as Himalayas,
as deep as Pangong Lake?
You are incarcerated souls
fluffed by a dream
of comfort and career.
Hollow men; not like ants or bees
for whom the colony matters,
without colony, where is the heart to be…

Pretenders

Swirling moth,
keeping to the light path,
do not light up like mottled butterflies.

> Fireflies encircling trees;
> they are the torch to themselves
> but not a luminous acre.

Singing cicadas in tombs,
may be the hum in spectral silence
but not the choir of hallelujah.

> Simulacra decorated
> in a mastery of yarn, they are different;
> they are not even weak metaphors of leaders.

Patriotism

Patriotism is a predator
that stalks with eyes of tricolour.

A paintbrush to pour colour
on the *tabula rasa* of mind,
wiped clean of history, experience and wisdom.

All that remains in the end,
"We" and "them",
"they" merge with us
when it suits,
"we" remain standing apart,
when their hearts are to be carved
to find a blackened soul
of a nation; as dark as charcoal.

Stifled Voices

Sutured stutter or sputter
drown the intent mixed with words.
Images stirred out of the raging sea
were declared dead metaphors.
The tongue which bled
deciphering the mayhem of time,
is now dead or buried?

Enlisted Soldier

Rank, id, uniform and bedrolls,
pay, leave and pension,
home travel and decoration
are the warranties for the brave.

Life of usual mendacities,
death of surrounded security,
but the certitude in between
are not the guarantees we came with.

Half-Deserted Streets and Muttering Retreat

One Whom I Taught the Alphabet

You are the little girl
whom I taught the alphabet.

Wish you can
edit my poems,
strike lines on my prose,
correct grammar and typos,
teach me painting,
explain differential equation,
and tone my point down.
Because you are so much better.
If only you live with its acceptance,
you are the little girl
whom I put to sleep with stories.
Wish you can spin stories
as you did always
until you fell silent without them.
Wish you can step into the sun,
laugh with friends,
converse like pattering rain,
which you forgot on a whim.
Because there is so much more
in the world of a little girl growing up
than being bottled in the room
where no abracadabra is chanted.

Is There a Second Chance?

After sixty years there is no second chance.
For you, chances are more, you've just begun.

What if you stand, walk and fall,
you will walk again and grow very tall.
Tall you have already become
tall in life you will grow up to.

You do not know, you can't see that far
I can see, look back from afar.

Everyone comes with a to-do list, I had one.
I am busy decorating now, which is already done.

You have not started yet, you would go far.
But in everything you touch, as best as you want to be.
Just desire for it, the door will open,
forget about getting tired or gone.

Don't kick the door closed,
it would open again and again,
because your chances are so much more.

Geriatrics

Old age,
the enveloped aura of draining life,
softer breath and weakening recall,
you can call it the enchantment of decay,
long slow fading of skin colour,
bones stiff as a rifle,
wrinkles appearing like unexpected guests.

Old age,
aches bother you, so does the water in your eyes,
images recede before you catch them.
Memory flits in the tousled world of chaos,
teeth disappear when gums bother you.

When is the deliverance then?
Now or in future?
It is the sediment of the past,
unsolved,unfathomed and unknown,
holds the salvation from the beginning
beyond time and
memory.

Loyalty

Is there any use
carrying a profligate on your left shoulder
and a patriot on your right?
You should stand still like a needle
stuck in perfect balance,
look like unmoving stations,
their visiting cards useless like old timetables,
but you can't move by their mutual agreements.

Smoking

Smoke can swirl away
and bring words into a misty life.
Substance abuse is fake news,
insurance of the underwhelmed
seeking the camphor of anodyne existence.

Cigarettes remind of
Doric columns in colonnade;
strong enough to support the roof
also to provide exit routes.

Light one and puff away,
you would be spotting words and God
but your mind will have to believe
and your pen will have to write.

Free or Trapped

Are photos trapped in the frame
or are you fettered in clicks?

Is breath locked in the body
or is the body chained in them?

Do stories stack inside the bag
or become breathing stories with sunshine?

Body or a trap, liberation or fetters,
get defined with air, light and breath
beyond containment in imagination.

Clichés

We grow into clichés
or time delivers us quickly
into their sanctity.
Without notice or alert,
they creep into our lives,
stay put as unobtrusive
as they can be.
Because we have no dream
of becoming anything
other than stilted, simple and ordinary.

A Lucifer is Born

A speaker hollers and hectors.
A polite clap usually follows.
Maybe a standing ovation,
a faint smile on his face
and a protruding chest,
he adores himself, a star is born.

A writer writes,
some felicitation follows,
his beaming smile
touches the inside of earlobes,
the publisher picks it up on a whim,
a star is born.

How much is polite, how much real?
How much will fade in palimpsest?
And how much will abide?
But a luminous Lucifer is born,
only he will have to wait for his fall.

Hyderabad Rocks

Boulders are periods,
commas and marks of
exclamation or interrogation,
sculpted in love,
seasoned in abandon,
they are bookmarks mottled by time,
condensed, heartfelt and sacred
like words in a quatrain,
waiting for the paintbrush
of imagination to consecrate them.

Stubble Burning

Untilled land was a metaphor
of languid recovery of tired earth.
But how do we imagine stubble burning?
Smoke wafting to cover the sky,
blocking the light like sun-lotion,
choking the city, making breathing difficult,
it is the mayhem of the lynch mob,
the living don't laugh,
the dead don't stir,
we are all dying without knowing.

An Unplanned Departure

(In memory of Sanjib Das)

All departures are either late or soon,
but how do you fix a name
when it is sudden without a blast,
a storm without a warning gust.

It came from nowhere.
Stared you in the eye and stared you down.
The mayhem that followed was not a whim,
it was finally the codicil of gloom.

Death didn't stalk,
it just came like an irritation,
made light of you
as you have done to many and so often.

Who knew that fruit
will fall without notice,
a stem will sever before anyone knew.
Was it real or just another of your little jests?

Now between dark and dark,
there is not even a quirky spark.
When we stand in the midst of night,
you have hurried into people's orality.

You are not there, you didn't sleep,
always around when conversation sweeps,
a quiet bird in flights you weave,
you are there; you didn't really leave.

Our Longings

Our longings are
anything but definite.
They balk at definitions,
their destinations shift
all the time.
Is it because they are rigged for
a long journey?

Hope, Not a Tattered Flag

Between Starshine and Day

We were dancing when the hive collapsed,
the colony dissembled,
Imidacloprid, the bees were drunk with,
they could not wiggle to point
where the nectar was,
one thought the dark hour
has set in and has come to stay.

The night was dark and deep,
it was almost as black as ink.
Who thought there is a time beyond
witchcraft, voodoo and sorcery?
But who knew it was passing,
it was only the time
waiting for the sun to burst forth
and we were to become a bridge
between starshine and the day.

Hope

Hope, like ficus,
can take root in nothing.
It just needs so little;
stones, a crumb of earth,
will do as an anchor
in a landscape of despondency.

Then it can grow skyward
with sunshine and air.
The enveloping darkness
a wee hour ago
becomes forgotten weeds
after a long winter.

Lifescape

Ours was a mutilated world
though the curtains fluttered
and the music flared.
We gathered flowers in the park
when the wind abducted leaves.

We were witnesses without speech.
Our eyes had tears
not cried out yet,
bowed head and lowered eyes,
shoulders drooping like
trees after the foliage,
we were like
hanging icicles.

Does it surprise you?
We were not devoured by hatefulness
nor shot down with their words
nor cut with dagger eyes.
Something always stood up,
when many kept trying,
we were not killed yet.

We were written down in history
with bitter twisted lies,
our soulful cries had hollowed us.
And we faced the onrush of terror,
cornering us without an escape route.
But into a daybreak we rise now
carrying the gifts of our ancestors.

Finally, time has no strength to demolish us,
in a sense, it came from us
not we from time.

Life at the End of the Tunnel

Hope is not just a warm, assuring glow
of looking forward,
nor is it heart-spun word- clouds clearing
or night disappearing,
for leaving the tribulations behind.
It is not just a new sunrise.

Even if truth drowns,
legions ready to make the
untruth devour the truth,
truths always wash ashore
not caring how deep they were buried.

Terror becomes a pantomime after a while,
like the birds who get bored of the scarecrow
or nonchalantly sit on the wire
not alive and long dead.

Hope is like a clay pot
baked in embers,
holding sharp pain
and gathering enough strength
to push back.

Acknowledgements

SOME POEMS IN this volume have appeared in poetry collections and a book by Penguin India. My grateful thanks are due to M.K Ajay, Manu Dash and Alvin Chang as four poems *Patriotism, Death of Civility, Dharma Sansad* and *The Oracle* appeared in the book *Hanging Moment* (2024). *Incomplete Voyages, False History* and *The Tragedy of Uttarakhand* were published in *Map of the Morning* (2023). *Breathless* and *Hope* were published in *Storms in Bones* (2025). The editors Manu Dash, M.K Ajay, Sabin Iqbal and Pramudith D. Rupa Singhe must be profusely thanked for selecting them for publication. Special thanks are due to Manu Dash for publishing *No Earthly Colour Will Change* in Penguin India's volume *The Big Book of Odia Literature.*

Thanks galore to Ravi Singh, Chief Editor of Speaking Tiger for providing a caring home for the book. Swati Daftuar of Speaking Tiger also deserves my grateful thanks as the Editor of the volume. I must record my gratitude to early readers of these poems. Ashok Lavasa, Jaishree Mishra, Mandira Ghosh, Amarandra Khatua and Ram

Shankar Nanda not only painstakingly went through them but also suggested some changes which leave the poems much improved.

I owe a special word of thanks to my wife Sanghamitra and my daughters Sanjana and Sukanya for continued support and encouragement. It will be a remiss on my part if I don't mention my co-writer Joey, my golden retriever who has been a constant company when I write.

9 789363 365186

Printed at Repro India Ltd.